Animals and Their Habitats

Level 3
Book 3

Columbus, OH

SRAonline.com

 SRA

Send all inquiries to this address:
SRA/McGraw-Hill
4400 Easton Commons
Columbus, OH 43219

ISBN: 978-0-07-610845-9
MHID: 0-07-610845-7

1 2 3 4 5 6 7 8 9 DBH 13 12 11 10 09 08 07

Table of Contents

SRA Decodable Stories

Bats

by Curtis Brinkman
illustrated by Meryl Henderson

Decodable Story 18

McGraw Hill SRA

Columbus, OH

1

Bats! These strange flying animals frighten some kids and amaze others. One thing is apparent. Not many kids think bats are boring!

Yet, there are things kids do not understand about bats. And some things that kids think about bats are just wrong.

Here are bat facts that you might like to know and share.

Bats are not birds.

Bats fly, so they must be birds. Right? Wrong! Bats are mammals.

- Birds have feathers. Mammals have fur or hair.
- Mammals are born live. Birds hatch from eggs.
- Mammals give milk to their babies. Birds do not.

And birds can fly, but mammals cannot—except for bats! That's why bats are amazing.

Bats are not rodents.

Some kids think of bats as flying rats or mice. Rats and mice are rodents. Rodents are little mammals with strong teeth. Squirrels, beavers, and gophers are rodents, too, but bats are not.

Here is a surprise: Bats are more like apes and chimps than rodents!

Bats are not blind.

You have heard the phrase, "as blind as a bat." Yet bats are not blind. Bats see well. But bats also send sound waves as they fly. These sound waves reflect off things. These waves help bats find and catch insects at night. For bats, sound waves are even better than sight!

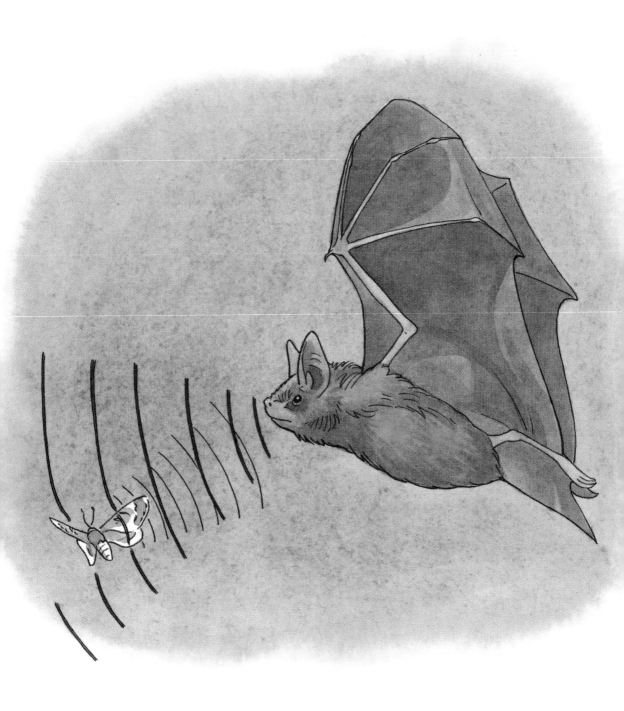

Bats hide well.

Do bats live near you? Bats might, but it is hard to tell. Bats sleep out of sight in daytime. Bats fly and hunt for bugs at night.

Where can bats sleep? Bats can doze in barns, caves, high up in trees, or under bridges. And bats don't lie down to sleep. Bats sleep hanging upside down.

Bats help people and habitats.

People need bats. Why? Bats eat lots of bugs. Some bugs harm farmers' crops.

Bats live in most habitats. And bats help each habitat that they live in. In some places, bats are like bees. Bats help plants grow.

And bats can help you. How? The next story will tell more.

More Bats

by Ella Cherup
illustrated by Meryl Henderson

Decodable Story 19

SRA

Columbus, OH

A gentle wind was blowing. "The breeze feels nice," said Cody.

"Yes," agreed Joan. "A breeze after a slow, long rain is refreshing."

Cody and Joan looked at a meadow next to Joan's house. There were little puddles of water here and there. "But those puddles frighten me a bit," Cody admitted.

"Puddles frighten you? Why?" asked Joan.

"Puddles are places for bugs," said Cody. "Insects lay lots of eggs in puddles. Then more bugs hatch and grow. And the bugs are bad ones. They bite people!"

"I know about bugs and puddles," said Joan. "But the same puddles do not frighten me."

"Why not?" asked Cody.

"I will show you," replied Joan.

Joan led Cody to the side of her house. She showed him an odd-looking box. It was on a pole next to an oak tree. "Do you know what that is?"

"No," said Cody.

"It is a bat box," explained Joan.

"A *bat* box!" said a surprised Cody.

"Yes, it is made from cedar lumber," said Joan. "Bats like cedar."

"Bats!" said Cody. The term stuck in his throat. "You mean those creepy little things with wings?"

Joan smiled. "Yes," she said.

"I know why people have bird houses," said Cody. "But why would you have a bat box?"

"My dad made it," Joan said. "He hung it so bats might live here."

Cody was shocked. "Did it work?" he asked.

"Yes," said Joan. "An entire bat colony lives in the box."

"That means loads of bats! Why?" asked Cody. He looked a little afraid. He slowly backed away from the pole.

"Well, do you know what bats eat?" asked Joan.

"No," said Cody.

"Bugs!" smiled Joan. "A bat eats 500 bugs in a short time. A bat colony eats bugs all night."

"Your bats protect you from meadow puddles!" Cody said.

"Yes," said Joan. "Our bats will eat those bugs."

Cody said, "That means I can like bats."

Joan smiled. "Unless you are a bug!" she said.

Condors

by Ella Cherup
illustrated by Meryl Henderson

Decodable Story 19

Columbus, OH

This story tells about another animal that helps humans. Without human help, this huge bird would not have survived.

Some people argue that a condor is an ugly-looking bird. Why? It has fluffy feathers all over its body. But its head looks like it has been shaved. That makes a condor's head seem too small. Plus the condor's face is often pink, red, or blue. In the middle of that face is a huge, odd-looking beak.

Yet when a condor flies, people change their minds about its looks. It is the biggest bird in the United States. Its wings stretch nine to ten feet apart. The undersides of its wings are white, outlined by black.

Up in the air, a condor is an incredible sight. It often seems to fly without working at it. It just seems to float.

Long ago, people called the condor by another name. They called it the thunderbird. The condor seemed so big that when it flapped its wings, it could make thunder! Few can deny how amazing the thunderbird looks flying high up in the sky. People continue to think that the condor stands for strength.

In its habitat, a condor has real value. A condor does not kill animals to survive. It eats animals that have died! That sounds yucky, but it's good. Condors help keep our world clean.

And each condor can help the world for a long time. Some condors live sixty years.

Yet for a while, not many condors had a chance to live that long. We humans hurt their habitat. We hurt condors. Condors came close to dying out. In the 1980s, just a few of these large birds were left.

Humans harmed condors, but humans also helped them. In the 1980s, a plan was started to rescue condors.

That rescue plan continues. Now, in cliffs high in the air, male and female condors sit on eggs and wait for condor babies to hatch. We wait, too. We want condors around for a long time.

Strange Stuff

by Tony Parker
illustrated by Meryl Henderson

Decodable Story 20

Columbus, OH

Bats and condors are strange animals. But most animals are strange. Take ducks, for example. Ducks have feathers, wings, webbed feet, and beaks. Their feathers can be bright and loaded with waxy liquid. A few ducks even have beaks with teeth!

Ducks are quite a sight! But when you think about it, ducks are just right. Why?

Ducks need those strange parts to survive. Ducks need webbed feet to help them swim. Feathers and waxy liquid are like a raincoat. They keep ducks warm and dry.

Beaks help ducks get things to eat. Some ducks need teeth to catch fish! Bright feathers help ducks find mates. Ducks need wings to fly to warm weather in winter.

Animals have bodies that help them survive. Look at the toad. It has bumps all over its body that help it hide. The toad looks like a rock by roads.

The bumps are dry unless an animal attacks the toad. Then, a liquid flows from the bumps. The liquid hurts the attacking animal, but that animal will not die.

Camels do not have bumps. Camels have humps. Those humps store fat. Humps help camels survive a long time without drinking or eating.

Camels' wide feet are made for traveling on dry, soft sand. Camels' long lashes stop sand from blowing in their eyes. Camels can even close their noses to keep sand out!

All animals must eat to survive. The way some animals get things to eat is frightening. Take a python snake, for example. A grown python can be more than twenty feet long. It lies waiting for an animal. Its mighty body squeezes that critter to death. The python then slowly gulps down its entire victim!

Look at a goat's eyes. Do they have black circles in the center like yours? No. Goats' eyes have wide, yellow rectangles. They can seem frightening.

Those rectangles give goats better sight. They help goats eat at night. Those eyes help goats survive.

As you continue reading, you will learn about an amazing plant that can live for 200 years!

A Visit

by Ella Cherup
illustrated by Meryl Henderson

Decodable Story 21

Columbus, OH

Pretend we are visiting an Arizona desert habitat. Truly, the best time to go is on a spring morning. Summer is too hot. Spring is much cooler.

We should expect to see lots of sand in a desert. And we do! But the desert is also filled with amazing plants. In springtime, many plants bloom.

The biggest plant is the cactus. Our eyes zoom to a large one. It looms fifty feet up in the blue sky. It has blooms on it. These are creamy white with yellow centers. As this day grows hot, the blooms will close. By late June, they will not be around.

And look! Morning dew sits on the cactus.

35

The cactus is not smooth. It has two-inch-long spikes all over. They are called spines. Spines keep the cactus cool. They protect it from some animals, too.

A cactus does not need much rain. Its roots do not extend too far. But the roots soak up water when it rains. The cactus swells to store that water.

See those holes in the cactus. Birds flew here and made those. Animals use the cactus for food. Due to the fact that a cactus stores water, animals use it to get water, too.

Holes can harm a cactus. Fluid can ooze out. But a cactus can reduce that harm by sealing those holes closed.

Bees and bats drink nectar from cactus blooms. This helps the cactus. Bees and bats carry bits of pollen from one bloom to another. Pollen helps cactus seeds grow. Those seeds fall to the desert. Soon new cactuses grow!

A cactus can live a long time. A few may live as long as 200 years. That's the truth!

We should end our visit. Too bad we cannot stay. At night, a cactus is like a zoo. Animals, birds, and bugs visit it for food and drink. At night, we would see proof of how much desert life needs cactuses.

Next, read about kids who have fun using what they know about an animal and its habitat.

Migrating
Geese

by Tony Parker
illustrated by Lynne Avril

Decodable Story 22

Columbus, OH

Little Eva began flapping her arms slowly and smoothly. Sue watched her and grinned. "Eva, what are you pretending to be?" she asked.

"I am a goose," said Eva. "I am a goose on the loose!"

"I knew it!" said Sue. She began to flap her arms, too. "I am up in the blue sky, too."

Eva and Sue ran slowly around the yard. They passed the wading pool. Eva nodded to it.

"See the pond below us," yelled Eva.

Sue pretended the pool was a pond. "Yes," she yelled back.

"We just flew from there. It is our summer habitat. But now we are flying away," Eva told Sue.

"I know why," said Sue. "The weather is turning cool. Soon the pond will freeze!"

Eva ran fast and zoomed around Sue. She continued flapping her arms. "You are right, Goose Sue," she said. "We are migrating to our winter home."

"How many geese are following us?" asked Sue.

"Quite a few," explained Eva.

The girls ran a bit more. "I am the goose leader!" said Eva. "I rule!"

Sue smiled at her little sister. "Okay. I am following you!"

"We are flying over vast open lands," added Eva. "Let's swoop down for a closer look."

Both girls turned and dipped on one side. Eva led Sue through the garden sprinkler.

"We are flying through a strong storm," yelled Eva.

Both girls pretended the storm blew them up and down.

Then the girls flew along the sandbox. "See that patch below. It's a desert," yelled Eva.

"Do geese fly over deserts?" asked Sue.

"The truth is that I do not know," said Eva.

The sisters flew past Dad. He smiled. What were they doing? Their flapping arms were a clue. Dad played along. He called to the girls, "Excuse me, little goofy ducks, but it is noon. It's time for lunch."

Eva stopped flapping. "Dad! We are not goofy ducks. We are goofy geese!" she said.

Sue chuckled. "That is true!"

Dad and Eva chuckled, too.

Introduction to Decodable Stories

Getting Started

Lesson	Decodable Story	Sound/Spelling Correspondences	High-Frequency Words Introduced
Day 1	**1** Nat, Nan, and Sam	/s/ spelled *s, ss* /m/ spelled *m* /t/ spelled *t, tt* /d/ spelled *d* /n/ spelled *n* /h/ spelled *h_* /a/ spelled *a*	hand, high, watch
Day 2	**2** A Pal	/l/ spelled *l* and *ll* /b/ spelled *b* /p/ spelled *p* /k/ spelled *c, k* /r/ spelled *r* /i/ spelled *i*	land, last, still
	3 Help	/f/ spelled *f* and *ff* /g/ spelled *g* /j/ spelled *j* /ks/ spelled ■*x* /o/ spelled *o* /e/ spelled *e, _ea_*	head, next, plants, turned
Day 3	**4** Fast Sam	/w/ spelled *w_* /kw/ spelled *qu_* /v/ spelled *v* /y/ spelled *y_* /z/ spelled *z, zz, _s* /u/ spelled *u*	hear, until
	5 Stars	/ch/ spelled *ch* /th/ spelled *th* /sh/ spelled *sh* /hw/ spelled *wh_* /ar/ spelled *ar* Closed syllables	above, night
Day 4	**6** Midge	/j/ spelled ■*dge* /k/ spelled ■*ck* /ch/ spelled ■*tch* /ng/ spelled ■*ng* /nk/ spelled ■*nk* Review /ks/ spelled ■*x* Schwa Review short vowels; closed syllables	children, move, second
	7 Fran and Ann	/er/ spelled *er, ir, ur,* and *ear*	earth, hard
Day 5	**8** Tell Your Pals	/or/ spelled *or, ore* Review /ar/ spelled *ar*	more, school, than
	9 Riddles	Syllable *–le* Schwa + /l/, including words with *el,* *il, al*	answer, thought
	10 Fran's Story	Review	other, story, things

Unit 1 Friendship

Lesson	Decodable Story	Sound/Spelling Correspondences	High-Frequency Words Introduced
Lesson 1	**11** Vic's Big Chore	/ā/ spelled *a* and *a_e* /ē/ spelled *e* and *e_e* /ī/ spelled *i* and *i_e* /ō/ spelled *o* and *o_e* /ū/ spelled *u* and *u_e*	back, close, time, while
Lesson 2	**12** Gem Is Missing	/s/ spelled *ce, ci_* /j/ spelled *ge, gi_*	home, large, name
Lesson 3	**13** More Clover	Review	change, most, talk
Lesson 4	**14** On a Train	/ā/ spelled *ai_, _ay* /ē/ spelled *ee, ea, _y, _ie_, _ey*	city, each, face, near, through
Lesson 5	**15** Bike Races	/n/ spelled *kn_* /r/ spelled *wr_* /f/ spelled *ph* /m/ spelled *_mb* /s/ spelled *_cy* /j/ spelled *_gy*	also, years
Lesson 6	**16** Too Cold?	Review	air, such

Unit 2 Animals and Their Habitats

Lesson	Decodable Story	Sound/Spelling Correspondences	High-Frequency Words Introduced
Lesson 1	**17** Bats	/ī/ spelled *_igh, _ie, _y*	even, might, need, trees
Lesson 2	**18** More Bats	/ō/ spelled *oa_, _ow*	house, same, side
Lesson 3	**19** Condors	/ū/ spelled *_ew , _ue*	feet, often, without, world
Lesson 4	**20** Strange Stuff	Review	almost, eyes, part
Lesson 5	**21** A Visit	/o͞o/ spelled *oo, u, u_e, _ew, _ue*	end, should
Lesson 6	**22** Migrating Geese	Review	along, began, following

Level 3 High-Frequency Words

above	earth	house	other	than
air	end	land	paper	things
almost	enough	large	part	thought
along	even	last	plants	through
also	ever	letters	point	time
answer	eyes	might	same	took
back	face	more	school	trees
began	feet	most	second	turned
between	following	move	set	until
book	hand	name	should	watch
change	hard	near	side	while
children	head	needas	still	without
city	hear	next	story	words
close	high	night	such	world
each	home	often	talk	years

Level 2 High-Frequency Words

again	eight	laugh	picture	thank
always	fall	learn	place	these
animal	far	light	play	those
another	fast	live	please	three
ate	find	made	pull	today
because	first	many	read	try
been	fly	may	round	under
best	found	much	run	upon
better	full	must	say	us
black	funny	myself	seven	use
both	gave	never	show	warm
bring	give	new	sing	wash
buy	goes	off	small	water
carry	great	once	soon	which
clean	grow	only	sound	white
cold	has	open	start	who
does	hold	our	stop	why
done	hurt	own	tell	wish
draw	keep	people	ten	work
drink	kind	pick		write

Level 1 High-Frequency Words

about	come	how	one	too
after	day	if	or	two
an	don't	into	over	very
any	every	its	pretty	walk
are	five	jump	put	want
around	four	just	red	water
ask	from	know	ride	way
away	get	like	right	well
before	going	long	saw	went
big	good	make	six	where
blue	got	me	sleep	will
brown	green	my	take	would
by	has	no	their	yellow
call	help	now	them	yes
came	here	old	this	your

Level K High-Frequency Words

a	could	her	on	they
all	did	him	out	to
am	do	his	said	up
and	down	I	see	was
as	for	in	she	we
at	girl	is	some	were
be	go	it	that	what
boy	had	little	the	when
but	have	look	then	with
can	he	of	there	you